HAL LEONARD PIANO LIBRARY

SONATINA ALBUM
CLEMENTI, KUHLAU, DUSSEK, AND BEETHOVEN

9 Sonatinas

Edited and Recorded by Jeffrey Biegel

To access companion recorded performances online, visit:
www.halleonard.com/mylibrary

Enter Code
5431-4188-5180-3753

On the cover:
The Song
by Albert Anker
(1831-1910)

ISBN 978-1-4234-0509-2

G. SCHIRMER, Inc.

DISTRIBUTED BY

HAL•LEONARD® CORPORATION

7777 W. BLUEMOUND RD. P.O. BOX 13819 MILWAUKEE, WI 53213

Copyright © 2007 by G. Schirmer, Inc. (ASCAP) New York, NY
International Copyright Secured All Rights Reserved

Warning: Unauthorized reproduction of this publication is
prohibited by Federal law and subject to criminal prosecution.

www.musicsalesclassical.com
www.halleonard.com

CONTENTS

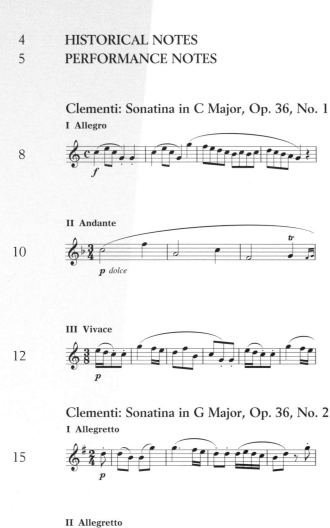

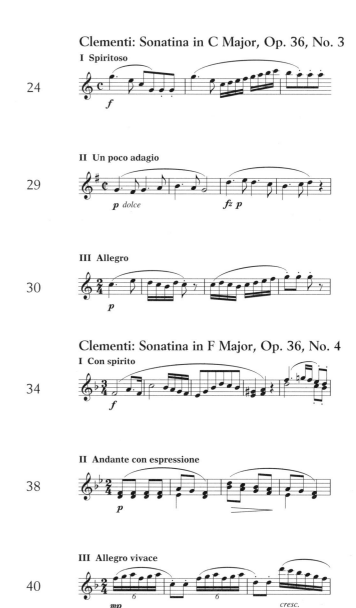

The price of this publication includes access to companion recorded performances online, for download or streaming, using the unique code found on the title page. Visit **www.halleonard.com/mylibrary** and enter the access code.

HISTORICAL NOTES

THE SONATINA

The cherished sonatinas of this album, written some 200 years ago, remain favorites of students and teachers. They offer a lively introduction to the more complex cousin of the sonatina, the "sonata." Literally meaning a "little sonata," the sonatina is structured in such a way that it resembles a scaled-down version of the larger musical form.

Sonatas have existed for over 400 years, but truly came to prominence in the late 18th century with the masterworks of Haydn, Mozart, and Beethoven. Early examples from the 17th century more closely resembled suites, often comprised of a set of dance movements. Sonatas from this period were most often written for small instrumental ensembles. The solo keyboard sonata emerged prominently in the 1740s with the works of Domenico Scarlatti and Carl Phillip Emanuel Bach, the latter of which often employed a three-movement form (fast-slow-fast) that would eventually become the ideal for the Classical sonata.

Muzio Clementi

The term "sonata" describes a particular compositional design beginning in the Classical period, and is sometimes used as the title for pieces that follow this design, or "form." Generally speaking, in a sonata-form movement, there are three large sections. In the first, a musical idea or "theme" is stated, sometimes followed by a secondary musical theme. This section is called the "exposition." Then, the main theme is developed, or expanded in various different keys. Often the theme is dissected into smaller fragments of itself in this section, known as the "development." The theme returns in its original key, intact, in the "recapitulation." This return of the theme is often noticeable to the listener, and is a musically satisfying moment in the composition.

A sonatina resembles the sonata but is a smaller-scale piece. The sonatina often has a short exposition section, wherein one or two main musical themes are presented. The development section is very short or is altogether omitted, with the return of the theme or recapitulation also being shorter than in a sonata.

Sonatas in the Classical period, the time during which most of the pieces in this volume were written, typically had three or four movements. The first movement (the one that expresses itself in "sonata form") often has a lively tempo, followed by a second movement in a slower tempo, sometimes followed by a short dance movement, and a final movement set again in a quick tempo. The sonatinas of Clementi, Dussek, and Kuhlau tend to follow this formula, although some are shortened to only two movements, as are those of Beethoven. The fewer movements are in keeping with the idea of a "little sonata," or sonatina.

The sonatina figured most prominently in the late Classical era. These master composers often wrote sonatinas for their students as teaching pieces, as well as writing more complex works for the piano such as sonatas and concertos—often as performance vehicles for themselves. Beethoven and Clementi, in particular, were known during their lifetimes as formidable pianists, often participating in the flamboyant competitions that were so popular in their day. Both men had a long line of students, some of whom—such as Beethoven's student, Karl Czerny—went on to write important teaching pieces themselves.

The sonatina form was rarely employed during the Romantic period as music grew into larger, and in many cases less formal, structures. This changed in the 20th century with piano works by Ravel (the *Sonatine*) and Bartók (*Sonatina on Themes from Transylvania*) as these composers and others moved away from Romantic excess toward the "neo-classicism" that influenced many composers of the 20th century.

—Susanne Sheston

PERFORMANCE NOTES

The continuing success of the *Sonatina Album*, published in *Schirmer's Library of Musical Classics* in 1893, shows that sonatinas remain vital teaching literature today. This new *Sonatina Album* includes works by Muzio Clementi, Friedrich Kuhlau, Jan Ladislav Dussek, and Ludwig van Beethoven. In compiling this edition with CD, I have focused on Clementi and Kuhlau, as they composed the largest numbers of sonatinas. There are pieces of varying difficulty, which make the volume attractive for students and teachers. These endearing sonatinas serve as stepping stones to the larger and more challenging masterpieces of the pianistic repertoire.

My editorial choices in this new Schirmer *Sonatina Album* reflect a "less is more" approach. I have added slurs and articulation only in places where I felt that some interpretive guidance would be helpful to students and pianists. The editorial markings correspond to my performances of the sonatinas on the accompanying CD, which I hope may also serve as a valuable and stylistically appropriate performance model. These works sound fresh and elegant whether played on an historical period instrument or on the modern piano. However, the many advances in the construction of the piano since these pieces were written enable us to draw upon a much wider range of expressive power than was available originally through varied articulations, touches, and subtle pedal techniques, all of which I encourage performers to explore and use in their own performances.

Articulation and Phrasing

The various touches and articulations described in quotations below are taken from Clementi's *Introduction to the Art of Playing on the Piano Forte*.

SLUR

Muzio Clementi instructed: *"When the composer leaves the LEGATO, and STACCATO to the performer's taste; the best rule is, to adhere chiefly to the LEGATO; reserving the STACCATO to give SPIRIT occasionally to certain passages, and to set off the HIGHER BEAUTIES of the LEGATO."* Clementi was one of several Classical-period composers who actively espoused a new school of "legato playing." Beethoven, who had a high regard for Clementi as a performer and composer, carried forward this new trend in his own performances at the keyboard.

STACCATO

Three types of short notes appear in these sonatinas.

Wedge:

"called in ITALIAN, STACCATO; denoting DISTINCTNESS, and SHORTNESS of sound; which is produced by lifting the finger up, as soon as it has struck the key"

Dot:

"or as they are marked thus

which, when composers are EXACT in their writing, means LESS staccato than the preceding mark (wedge); the finger, therefore, is kept down somewhat longer"

Portato:

"or thus

which means STILL LESS staccato: the nice degrees of MORE and LESS, however, depend on the CHARACTER, and PASSION of the piece; the STYLE of which must be WELL OBSERVED by the performer"

To carefully execute the proper touch of a particular passage, I sing the phrase aloud to evoke a vocal and aural sense of the piano. The arms, elbows, and wrists must be relaxed in order to create a singing tone. I stress the importance of phrasing melodic material over the bar line. How would the music appear if one eliminated the bar lines from the printed score?—the horizontal shape of the phrases would become readily apparent.

Dynamics

During the time these sonatinas were written the pianoforte did not have the large range of dynamics of the piano that evolved during the middle decades of the 19th century. During the 18th and early 19th centuries, *piano* would sound to us to be *pianissimo*, and *forte* would sound to us to be *mezzo forte*. To revise all dynamic markings by writing them one dynamic level softer than originally notated is unnecessary. Simply take this historic fact into consideration when performing the sonatinas (and any other works from the same period). Adhering exactly to the written dynamic notation on the modern grand piano can produce an overly Romanticized interpretation, which detracts from the intended classical style of sound.

Pedaling

Knee levers or foot pedals were new to the piano when the sonatinas in this volume were composed. Clementi's piano firm built an English Square Piano, circa 1796, which had a single damper pedal. Damper pedals might have been used to sustain the tone in slow movements or broken-chord material, since instruments of the early 19th century had a quicker decay of sound than modern pianos. In performing the works in this edition, I used pedal on long notes to sustain harmonic structure, connecting material when it seemed nearly impossible for the fingers to do so. Experiment with using quarter, half, and full pedal depending on the amount of sound you need to sustain. Consider also employing "finger pedaling"* to sustain accompanying harmonic material when possible.

Kuhlau: Sonatina in G major, Op. 55, No. 2: first movement, mm. 1-4

Use your ears to adjust the amount of pedal used depending on the instrument, and the room in which you are playing.

*Using the fingers to sustain the sound, rather than the damper pedal, giving the illusion that the pedal is being used without muddying the melodic material.

Fingerings

I advocate utilizing comfortable finger substitutions in this edition to maintain a pure legato phrase. This aids in creating a singing flow to the melodic material. I have inserted fingerings that are effective and easy for any size hand to employ. Certainly, teachers and performers should modify fingerings according to their hands.

Ornamentation

Although Clementi provided advice on ornamentation in his book, it was in flux during the period in which these sonatinas were written. As a result, there are no strict rules governing whether a trill starts from the principal note or the note above, or whether a grace note is performed on the beat or before. The choice should depend on the musical shape of the phrase. Similarly, the speed (i.e. rapidity) of a given ornament should be governed by the tempo and spirit of the piece.

The Appoggiatura

Clementi: Sonatina in C major, Op. 36, No. 3:
second movement, mm. 15-16

Clementi provides the following definition of the appoggiatura: *"The APPOGGIATURA is a GRACE prefixed to a note, which is always played LEGATO, and with more or less EMPHASIS; being derived from the ITALIAN verb APPOGGIARE, to LEAN UPON; and is written in a SMALL NOTE. Its LENGTH is borrowed from the following LARGE note and in GENERAL, it is half of its duration; MORE or LESS, however according to the EXPRESSION of the passage."*

The Turn

These ornaments should be played on the beat and generally within the harmonic context of the passage in which it appears. Clementi states: *"The TURN: The lowest note of every sort of turn is mostly a semi-tone."*

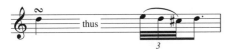

This is true of the example above, but there are examples of turns for which Clementi's suggestion does not necessarily provide a satisfactory answer. In measure 31 of Clementi's *Sonatina in F major, Op. 36, No. 4*, the turn could be performed satisfactorily with a G-natural or a G-sharp:

Clementi: Sonatina in F major, Op. 36, No. 4:
second movement, m. 31-32

The Slide

The slide appears in measures 31 and 34 of Beethoven's *Sonatina in G major*. Given the moderate tempo of this movement, I play the slide slightly before the beat, treating the notes of the slide as important melodic material. Singing this passage will help with the graceful execution of the ornament.

Beethoven: Sonatina in G major:
second movement, mm. 29-31

The Trill

Clementi offers his advice on the trill: *"The GENERAL mark for the shake is this **tr** and composers trust CHIEFLY to the taste and judgment of the performer, whether it shall be long, short, transient, or turned."* While Clementi preferred the upper note start for most trills, there are instances when the trill can begin on the principal note, most often when the trill is preceded by the note above. Suggestions for playing the trills are included in the edition. The number of oscillations in a trill may vary depending on the ability of the pianist, and the musical context of the passage.

Suggested Reading

Clementi, Muzio. *Introduction to the Art of Playing on the Piano Forte* (1801), ed. Sandra P. Rosenblum with New Introduction (1973). New York: Da Capo Press, 1974.

—*Jeffrey Biegel*

Sonatina in C Major

I

Muzio Clementi
Op. 36, No. 1

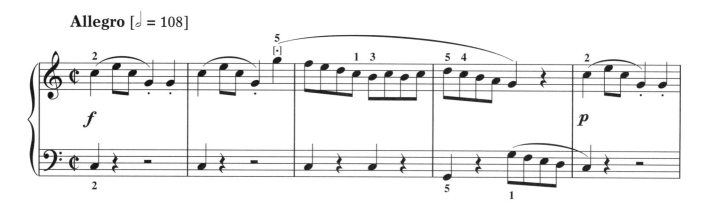

Copyright © 2007 by G. Schirmer, Inc. (ASCAP) New York, NY
International Copyright Secured   All Rights Reserved
Warning: Unauthorized reproduction of this publication is
prohibited by Federal law and subject to criminal prosecution.

II

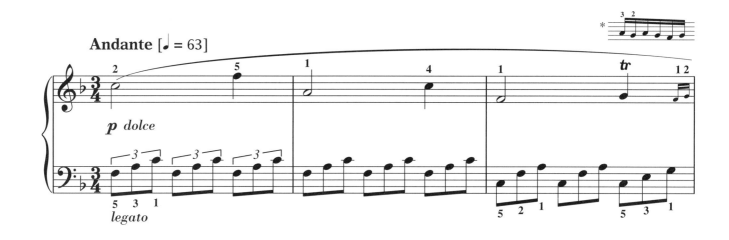

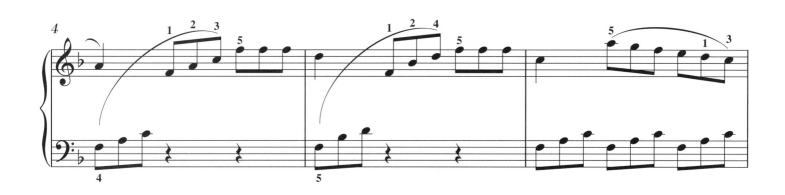

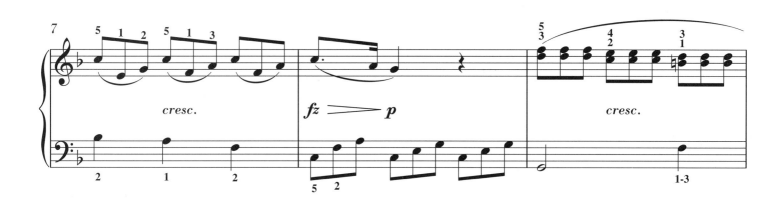

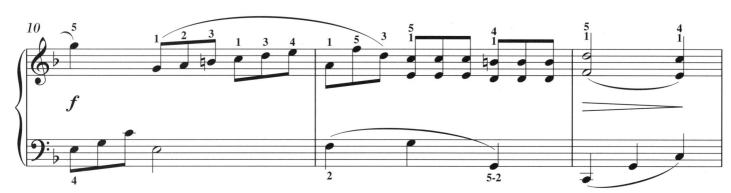

*This may also be played as an unmeasured trill.

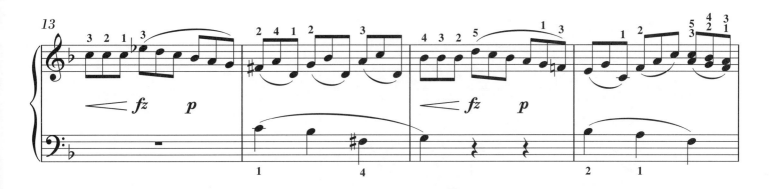

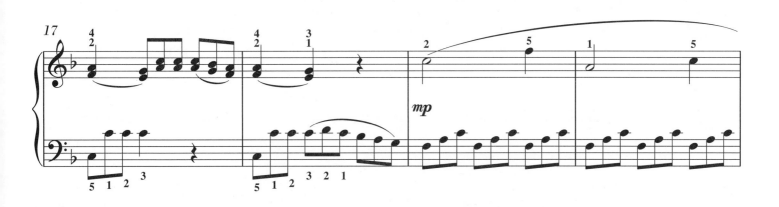

III

Sonatina in G Major

I

Muzio Clementi
Op. 36, No. 2

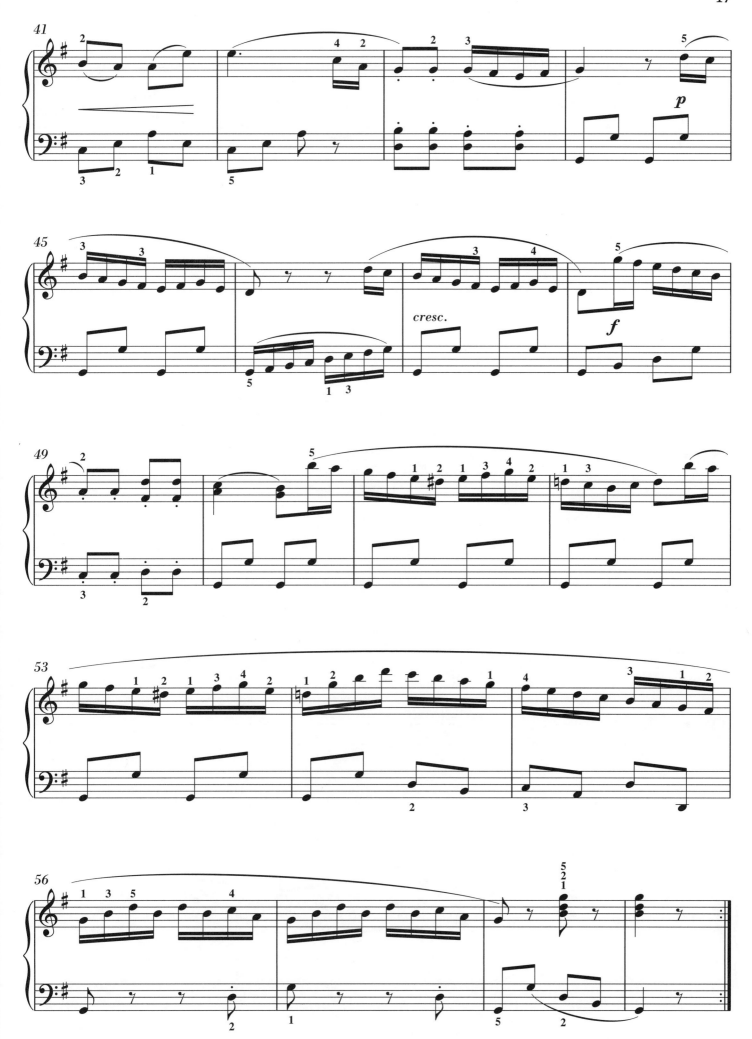

II

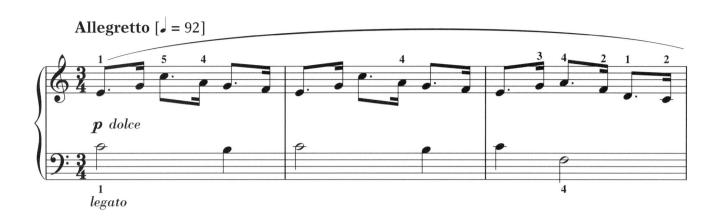

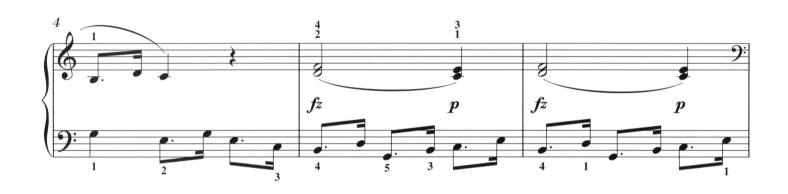

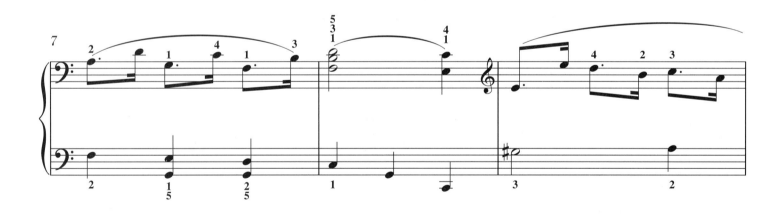

III

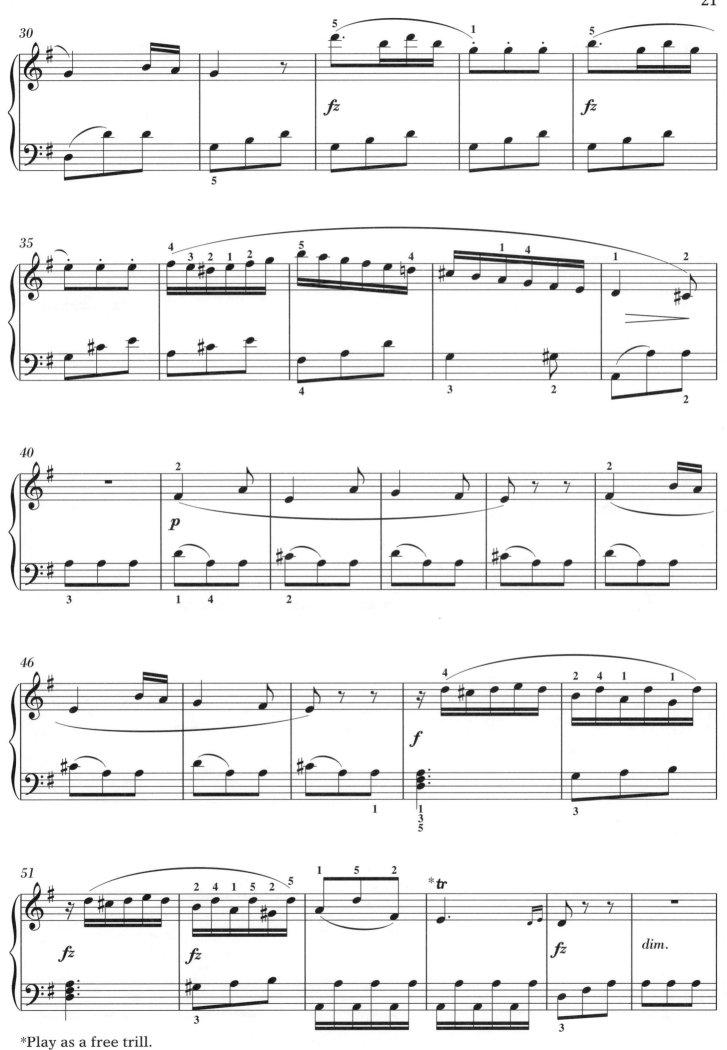

*Play as a free trill.

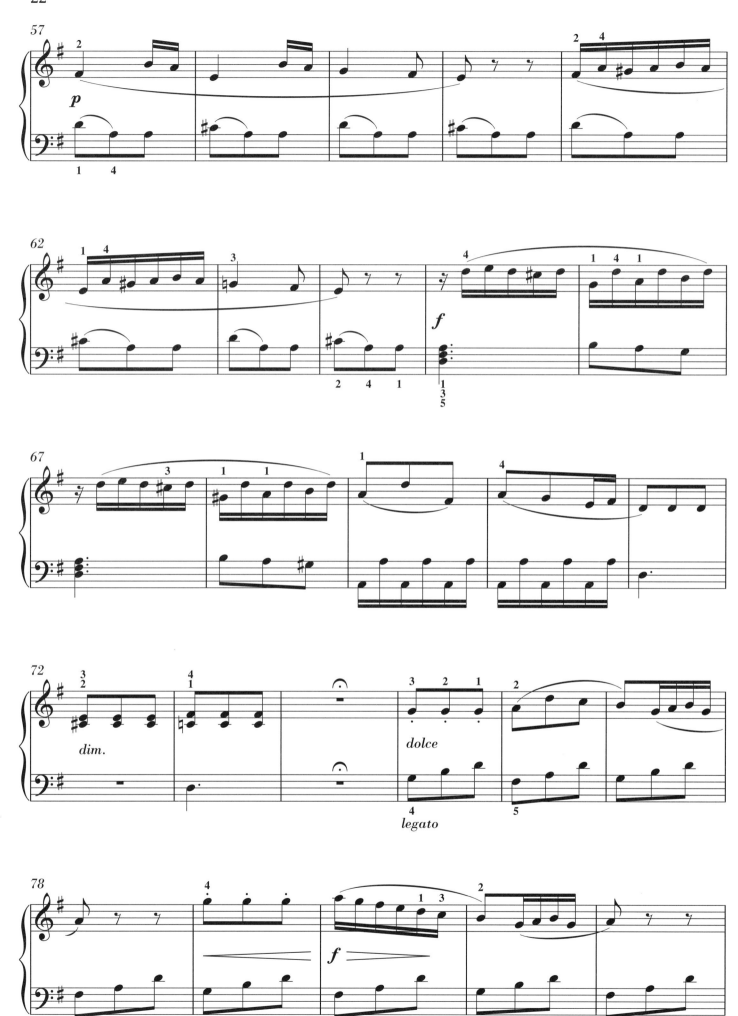

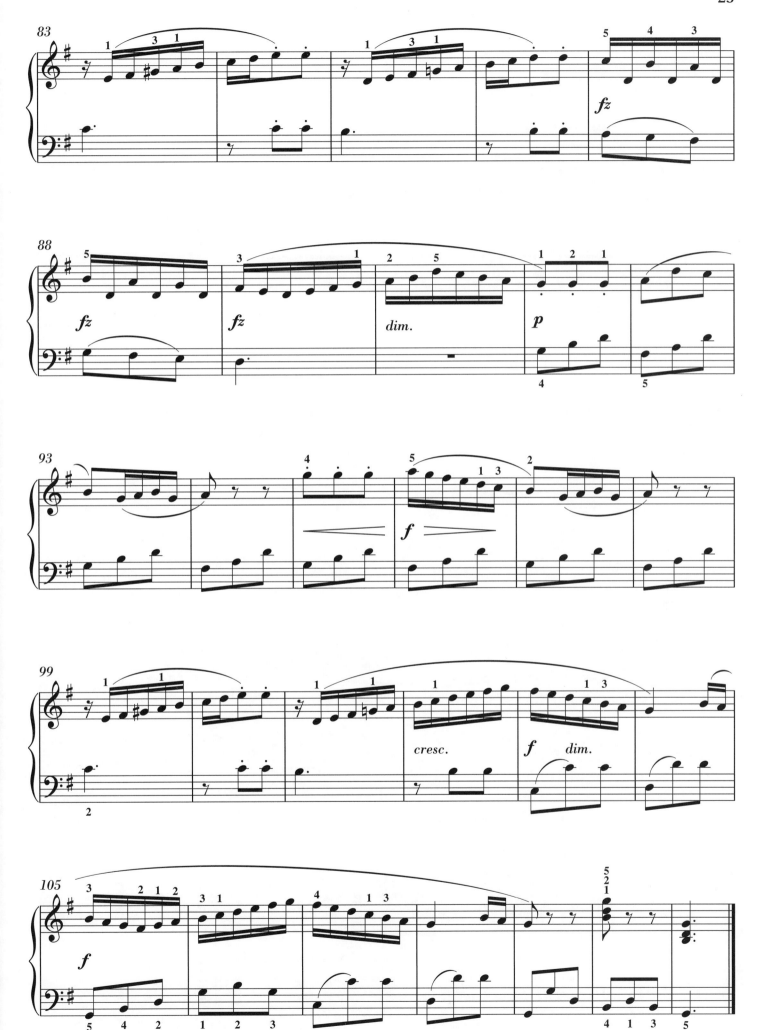

Sonatina in C Major

I

Muzio Clementi
Op. 36, No. 3

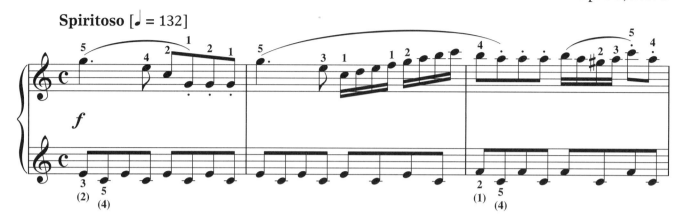

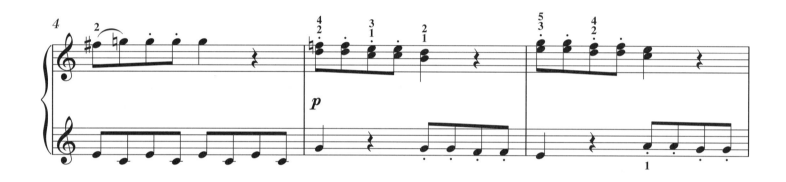

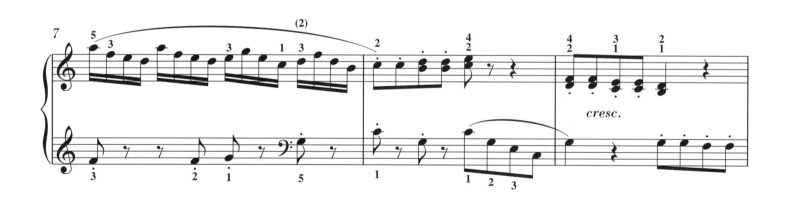

* optional

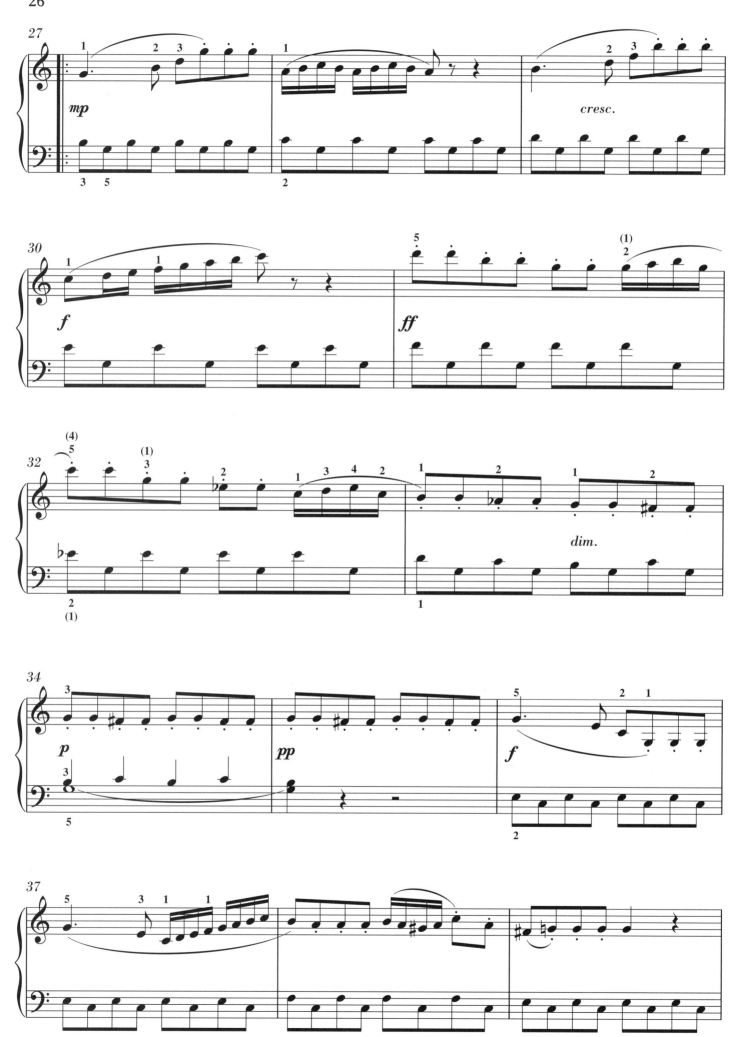

II

Un poco adagio [♩ = 88-92]

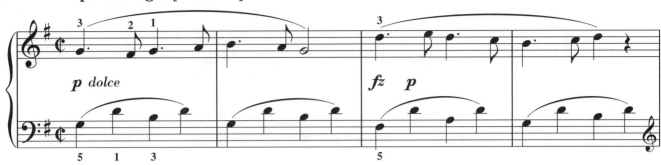

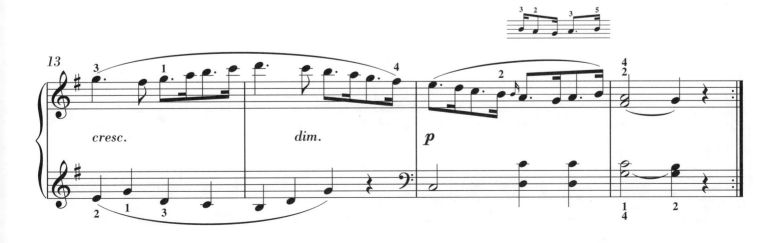

III

Sonatina in F Major

I

Muzio Clementi
Op. 36, No. 4

Con spirito [♩ = 126]

II

Andante con espressione [♪ = 104-112]

III

Rondo
Allegro vivace [♩ = 84]

Sonatina in G Major

I

Ludwig van Beethoven
Kinsky-Halm Anh. 5, No. 1

II

Sonatina in G Major

I

Jan Ladislav Dussek
Op. 20, No. 1

Allegro non tanto [♩ = 132]

*All notes with the accent ⸸ should be played very short, though as part of the melodic material.
Staccato indications exist in measures 17 and 19 only. These should be played lightly.

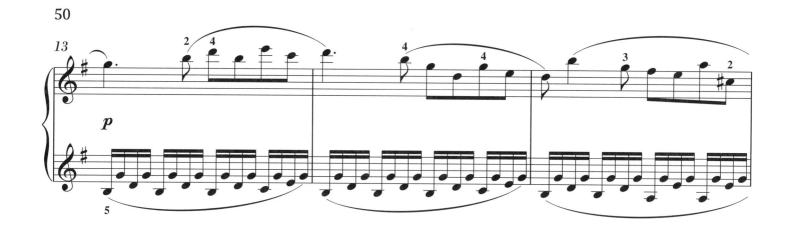

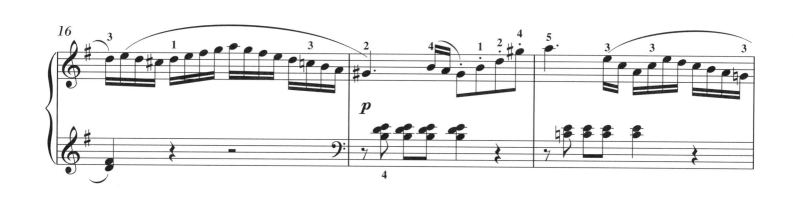

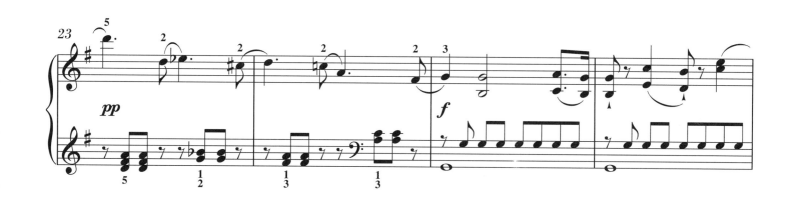

II

Rondo

Allegretto–Tempo di Minuetto [♪ = 126]

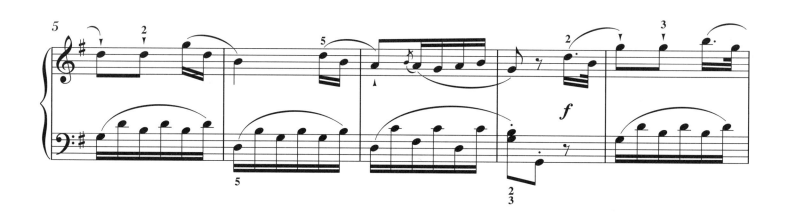

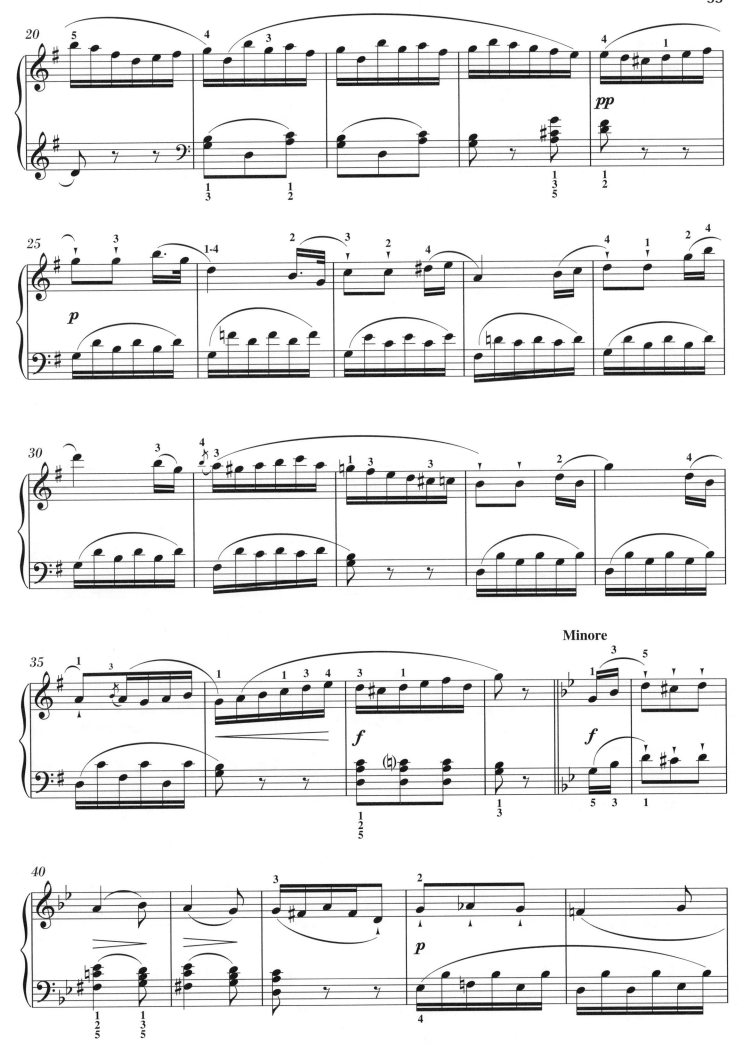

54

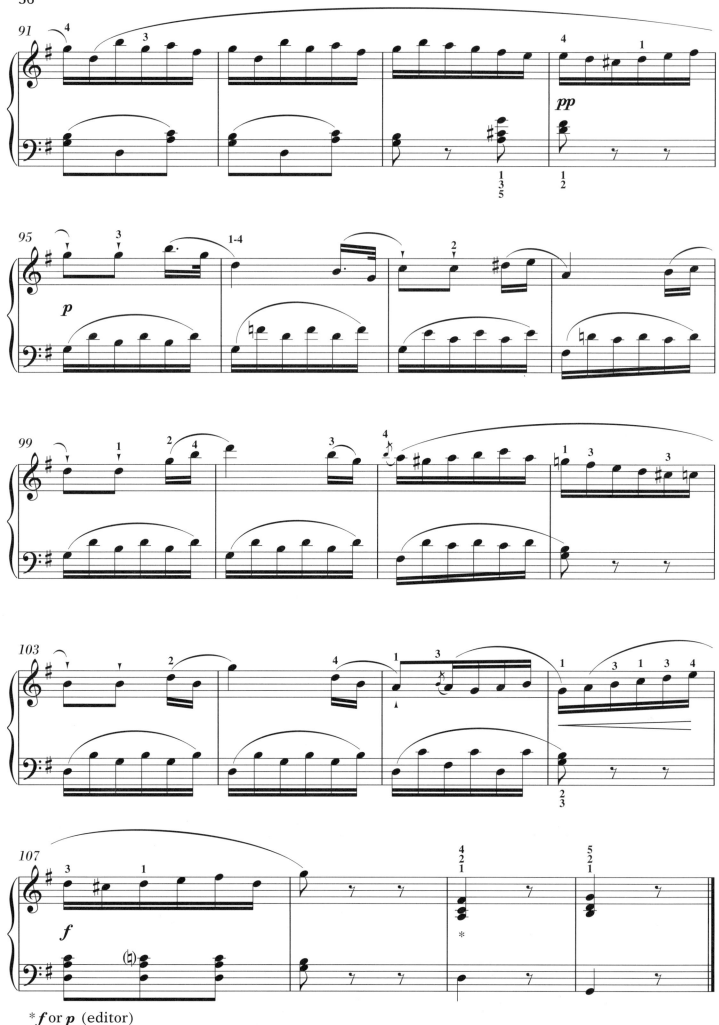

*f or p (editor)

Sonatina in C Major

I

Friedrich Kuhlau
Op. 55, No. 1

II

Sonatina in G Major

I

Friedrich Kuhlau
Op. 55, No. 2

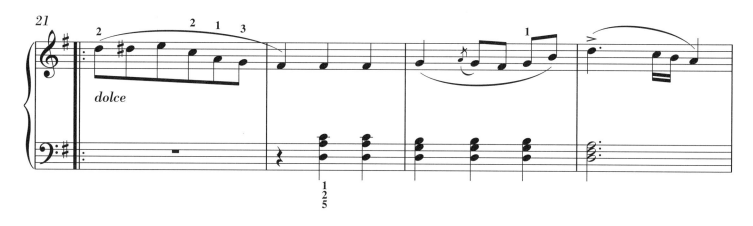

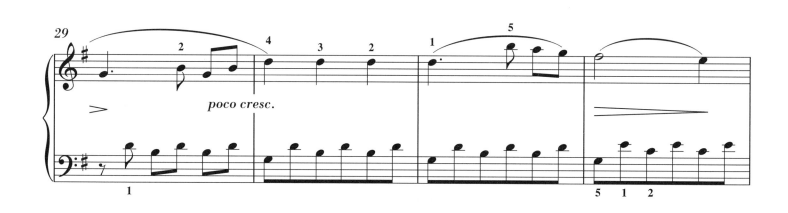

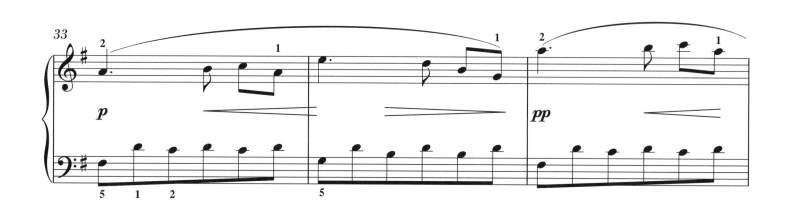

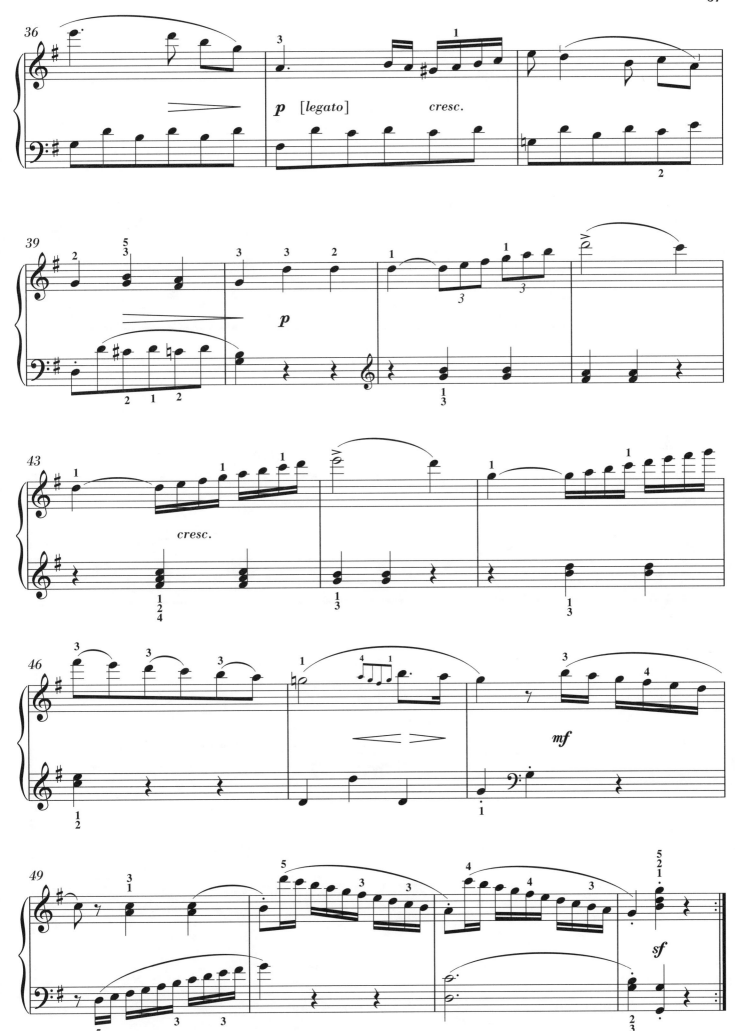

II

Cantabile [♩ = 69]

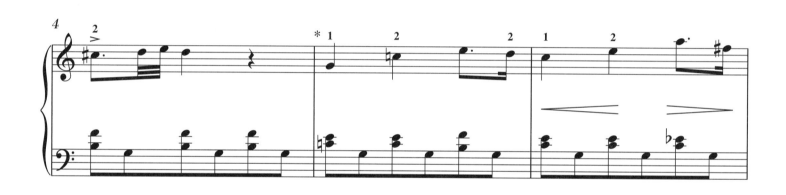

*Could be ornamented on the repeat.

III

Allegro [♩ = 126]

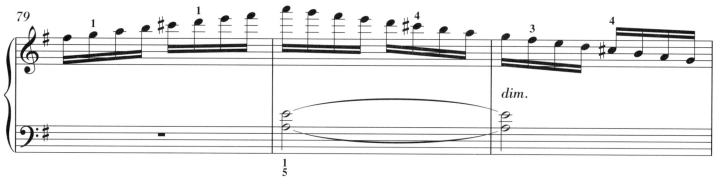

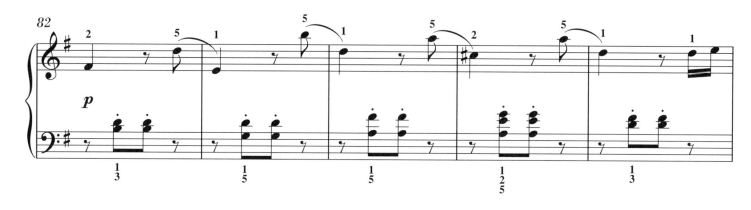

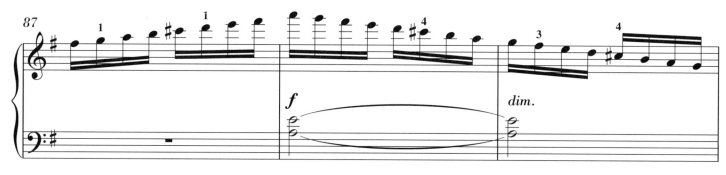

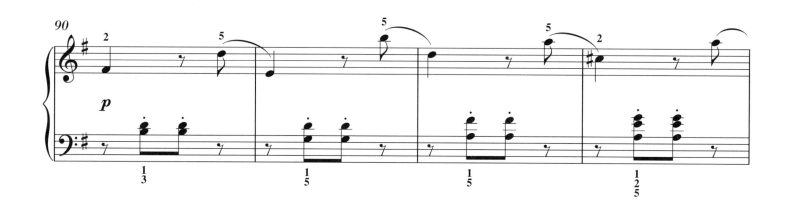

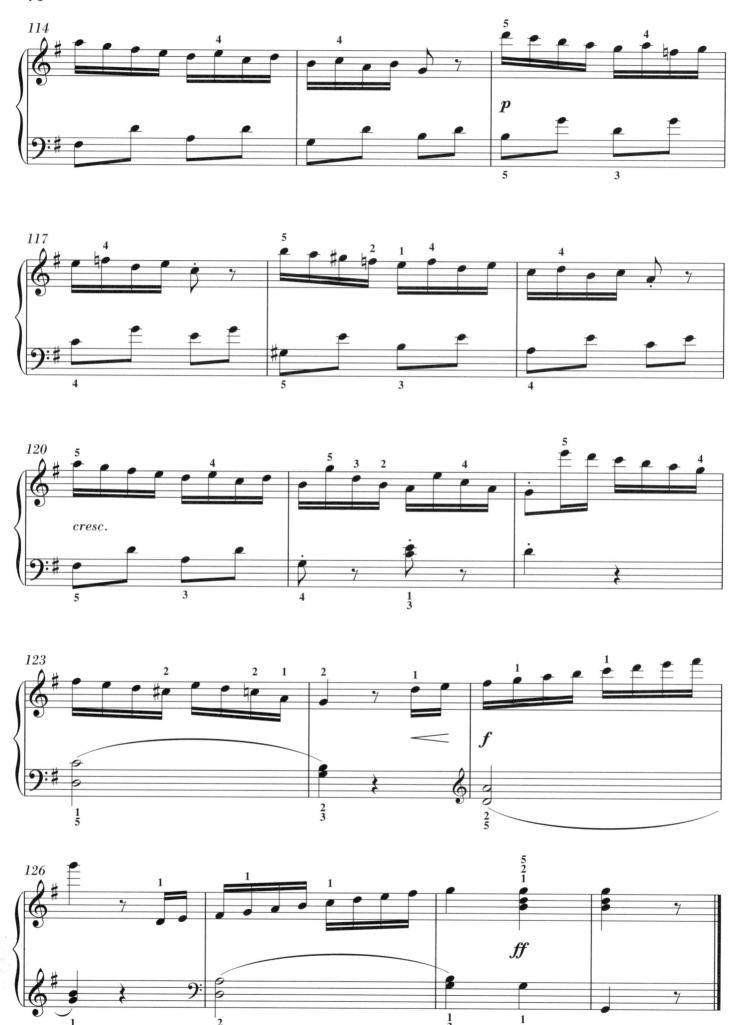

Sonatina in C Major

I

Friedrich Kuhlau
Op. 55, No. 3

Allegro con spirito [♩ = 132]

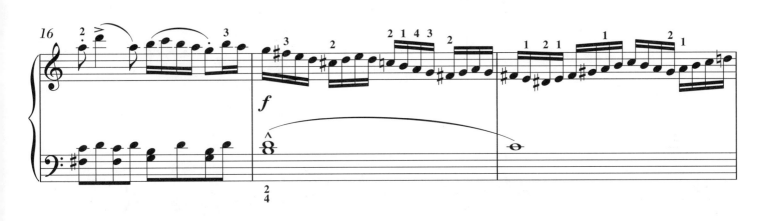

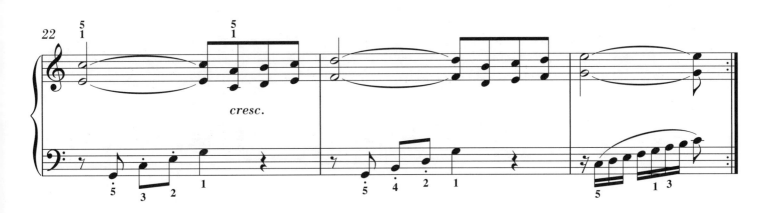

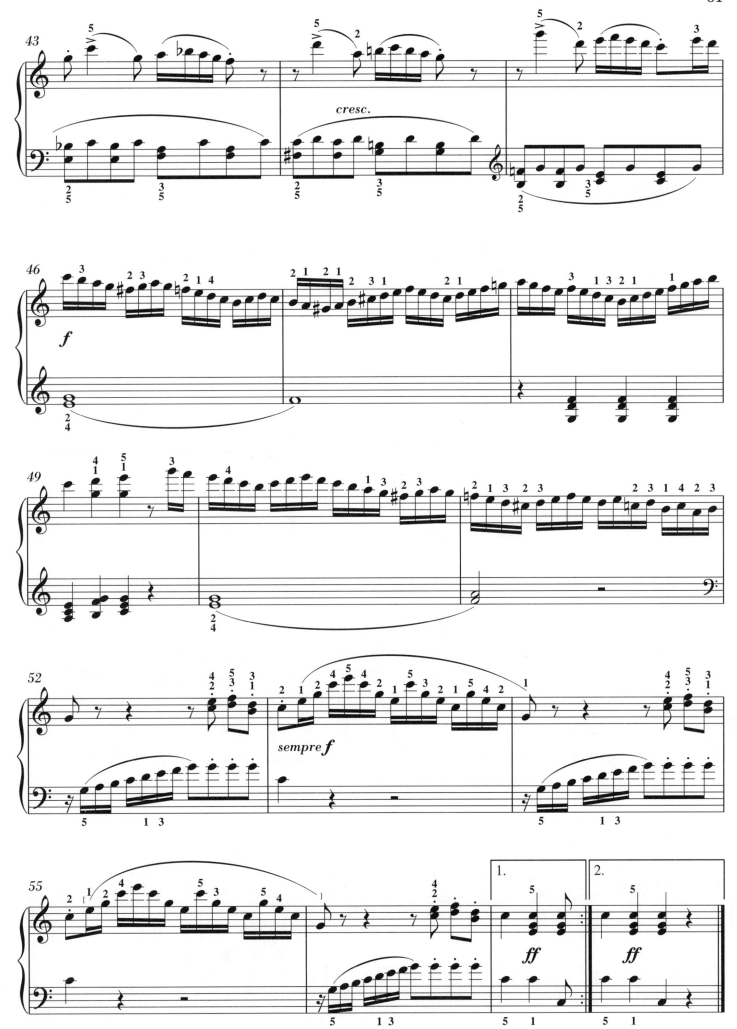

II

ABOUT THE EDITOR

JEFFREY BIEGEL

Leonard Bernstein said of pianist Jeffrey Biegel: "He played fantastic Liszt. He is a splendid musician and a brilliant performer." Biegel is one of today's most respected artists and has created a multi-faceted career as a pianist, composer, and arranger. His career has been marked by bold creative achievements. In 1997, he performed Gershwin's *Rhapsody in Blue* with the Boston Pops Orchestra based on the restored, original 1924 solo piano manuscript. He performed the first live internet recitals in New York and Amsterdam in 1997 and 1998. In 1999, he assembled a consortium of over 25 orchestras to celebrate the millennium with a new concerto *(Millennium Fantasy for Piano and Orchestra)* composed for him by Ellen Taaffe Zwilich. Charles Strouse composed *Concerto America* for Biegel, celebrating America and honoring the heroes and events of September 11, 2001. He assembled a global consortium to commission the *Concerto No. 3 for Piano and Orchestra* by Lowell Liebermann with performances scheduled in 2006-2008 with consortium orchestras. Biegel also arranged the *Symphonic Fantasies for Piano and Orchestra* based on four of Billy Joel's classical compositions from *Fantasies and Delusions.* These virtuosic transcriptions consist of four solo piano pieces, orchestrated by Phillip Keveren. Biegel recorded Leroy Anderson's *Concerto in* C with Leonard Slatkin conducting the BBC Concert Orchestra for a 2007 Naxos CD.

In addition to his concert activities, Biegel and his son, Craig, co-composed *The World In Our Hands,* reflecting the events of September 11, 2001 with a vision for hope and peace.

PianoDisc has released Biegel's recordings *Rare Gems of the Golden Age, Best of David Foster, Best of Leroy Anderson, Best of Josh Groban* in his solo piano arrangements, and a set of *Classical Carols* arranged by Carolyne M. Taylor. Additionally, he has recorded his solo transcription of the complete *Four Seasons* by Vivaldi, along with Grieg's *Suite in the Antique Style (after Holberg)* for Yamaha PianoSoft. Biegel recorded the world premiere of Lalo Schifrin's *Piano Concerto No. 2 - The Americas* with the Bayerischer Rundfunk (Munich Radio Orchestra) for the motion picture soundtrack *Something to Believe In.*

Jeffrey Biegel was the unanimous recipient of the First Grand Prize in the Marguerite Long International Piano Competition and First Prize in the William Kapell/University of Maryland International Piano Competition. He studied at the Juilliard School with Adele Marcus. Biegel teaches at the Conservatory of Music at Brooklyn College and the Graduate Center of the City University of New York.